Saccade Patterns

Deborah Meadows

Saccade Patterns

Deborah Meadows

BlazeVOX [books]

Buffalo, New York

Saccade Patterns by Deborah A. Meadows

Copyright © 2011

Published by BlazeVOX [books]

All rights reserved. No part of this book may be reproduced without
the publisher's written permission, except for brief quotations in reviews.

Printed in the United States of America

Book design by Geoffrey Gatza

First Edition
ISBN: 978-1-60964-006-4
Library of Congress Control Number 2011921086

BlazeVOX [books]
303 Bedford Ave
Buffalo, NY 14216

Editor@blazevox.org

publisher of weird little books

BlazeVOX [books]

blazevox.org

2   4   6   8   0   9   7   5   3   1

BlazeVOX

Other Works include:

How, the means (Mindmade Books, 2010)

Depleted Burden Down (Factory School, 2009)

Goodbye Tissues (Shearsman Press, UK, 2009)

involutia (Shearsman Press, UK, 2007)

The Draped Universe (Belladonna* Books, 2007)

Thin Gloves (Green Integer, 2006)

Growing Still (Tinfish Press, 2005)

Representing Absence (Green Integer, 2004)

Itinerant Men (Krupskaya Press, 2004)

"The 60's and 70's: from *The Theory of Subjectivity in Moby-Dick"* (Tinfish Press, 2003)

Acknowledgments

The author wishes to thank Guy Bennett whose Mindmade Books (Los Angeles) first published the segment *How, the means* as a chapbook. Thanks to editors Tony Frazer of *Shearsman Magazine*, Jennifer Stewart of *Compass: University of New Orleans online journal*, William Allegrezza of *Moria* who published earlier versions of some poems, and for the translation into Spanish of some poems by editors, William Allegrezza and Galo Ghigliotto in the forthcoming anthology *La Alteración del Silencio: Poesía Norteamericana Reciente* (Das Kapital Press, Santiago, Chile). Thanks also to Howard Stover, John Tranter, and Susan Schultz for conversations related to the project.

Portions of the section "where, a site index" derived, in part, from Wikipedia entries on Head-up display and Synthetic Vision system; while portions of "keep, a melodrama" owe to the *Compact O.E.D.,* to artwork entitled *Threadwaste* by Robert Morris, and to books: *Engines of Logic: Mathematicians and the Origin of the Computer* by Martin Davis, *Frank Zappa, Captain Beefheart and the Secret History of Maximalism* by Michel Delville, *Pi in the Sky: Counting, Thinking, and Being* by John D. Barrow, and *Primates and Philosophers: How Morality Evolved* by Frans De Waal.

Cover Art: "After Charles Mingus' *Better Git it in Your Soul*," a collaborative lithograph by Patrick Merrill and Deborah Meadows

for Howard

Contents

W. V. Quine: "To be is to be the value of a variable."

Saccade Patterns

Threadwaste

Everyone went there to be seen by someone.

Send six, or five, of your best.

Evening as a differential equation
        from here, barred in triple reveal,
loose change blocked from view.

The ripped out, free matter roughly torn
from tripods of western perspective, now
        only somewhat recognizable
lumped here, more garbage than sourcebook.

That some came from rolls...
fell a manufacturer's sortage plan—
        down, deft, voter-less. That impression
so negligently made recurs at what noise level?
Bent back, thin straw paper soggy
with it, grid to equidistance one from one another
so no conversation, disgruntled sub-vocalizing
makes jointure of pain, rip-off by degree
        saccade coverage where mitigation enters late.

As part of habitat gotten up to resemble savannahs

star-like
concerning a formal system, try to dance

meager drizzle in cement channel

no longer permitted to independent
observation: plaque, umbrellas, rote memorization

airplane overhead
headache from excess
light, too bright

operators yet improvability
marshals much evidence to illustrate arbitrary claims
carried out with finitary methods

others
others have forearm across brow
light, too bright
food, untouched

Dehiscence all over yourself

Each one and parts that belong are here.
A kid's thing to slam handles from table edge
to winked flight. Remember how weak
in association they are, you might say
our glue is stronger than our tape, spoons.
Subtracted out public square, long strings
of numbers crumble into play, constituent
material, liberty from intrusion, intractable
packets of zeros and onés, so imaging's interlace
if the spatula, set edge-down, originates *scrape* here
from coercive force, material recreation of life—
then no one-to-one dust-up, then where is the string
holding all strings, no terra cotta to weep more, weep less.

Opercula, fall off as they open

Poincaré: "I protest above all against the use of an infinite quantity as a *completed* one,
which in mathematics is never allowed."

            Strange combinations, some Justinian
plus Neptune, civil claim for addition, apse for infinite set,
mathematician in his prohibition against completion
that here is merely one of four mythic phases of the earth. It came out from
the insides of Mediterranean life, its gizzard a straw heap
vaguely donkey temperature, practice of rennet mostly local,
something not on paper, not a king-like god, so the other eye
exceeds the start
come round again swimming here, clothes weighted with water, from eye
a tiger-tined metal sinks, that is
negative from oarlocks' drip, undulate sheen of cathedral lights
recursive for now.

B: To claim abstract thought for apes? Primatologists have been burned too often.

A: What about math? With two hands, base 10 seems a bodily extension. How hard could that be?

how much computation possible without language?

eucalyptus caps (one-to-one correspondence, derive
			symbol for word-logic, other items
			for relations, i.e., if …, then …)

groundskeeper rakes them away

past addition
how to conceive of multiplication, observation of moon
in relation to solstice observation of aligned bar of sun,
sets of days → months → years

psychology of nuclear primate family imposed
        misrepresents set as complete

projection of eucalyptus caps
– what is "between" each one?
– how can infinite amount be in relation
                              to itself?
– why the ongoing puzzle of how 0, 1, 2
have unique properties?

So, start with something simple, base 10, what if one eu-cap for 10 digits,
then 10 eu-caps now represent 100 …

                    *

is the point to compress large quantities
into small items, so then, several small
items can be manipulated more handily,
yet the full result can be expressed
when called upon to all place values

B: Putting aside, for now, the problem of how we can determine presence of math-thinking in another species, in human population, the genetic diversity is so great we do see unusual math abilities in individuals here & there. Not clear though if same could be said for much reduced genetic diversity in apes.

eucalyptus caps fall here
(or call them eucalyptus pips,
or gumnuts in Sydney?)
made small piles, made rows,
made outlines of circle, barred zone
filled in circle, barred zone with same

man in green work shirt, rake,
            barrel on wheels

provide a solution
to the general problem reduced
                              to special case

it seemed I had ignored protocol
for greeting others, dropped
handful of eucalyptus cap

                    imagine:
a long tape of caps, from here,
along the length of habitat, down
the drainage gully then up to visitor
areas and beyond to parked cars, highway

and on, and on

and now imagine another set of same

what is the relation of the one to the other?

                              Imagine
if one set were stacked vertically
to the longitudinal one, curved here but not stretched?

Imagine the relation of one eu-cap horizontally
to one vertically, then at two-position vertically, etc.?

could other functions occur if along the horizontal
        one eu-cap meant quantities other than one?

man in green work shirt
rakes leaves and eu-caps
wheels away all counting materials
                            void, for now

think, hold image in mind of eu-caps
        let one stand for amount of fingers, two thumbs,
so sparse eu-cap collection here at base of tree, sixteen
        stands for sixteen (two hands)
        then, one hundred sixty

compact it all further?

        shadow of building, its tip, ends here
hands from here to base of building …

                              *

beam of light
through holes in paper tape

                              *

punched cards
for the Jacquard loom

the persistence of primate generosity
            in the face of adversity

repeated squares, crackers,
            tiles, swatches of paint
household ideas
grounded here

C: In serious literature, the charges of "sentimentality" and "animal story" are enough to foreclose this sort of exploration.

A: Yet writers often use language to image non-linguistic events as part of its means, no?

On seasonal change—

day-flies
feel it, visitors
their glandular smell

                         *

supposed to do my thing up here
            instead
I'll frame a question for them:

Could we think of variable extinction?

                         *

                              consequently
No more birth of veal)

how will thought halt,
where's a single groan

installed?

Histolytically speaking

This precise eucalyptus bark peels down—
it's how the tree narrows down possibility

yet placed here, they must adore
the equation: hinge between
here and there, zero and quadratic items,
unripe earth and fraught sky, loose confederacy toward
a skimpy democratic plan.

Not defeated by singularity, shown in how it makes more—
          who will inscribe this life
          somewhere, with what means?

Who would inscribe either random
or systematic thoughts of a primate?

   :How can one soliloquize over anonymity? Is it the tragedy of lost mathematic insight?

   :At pure end, the odd paradox of how it's most precious as lonely discovery yet simultaneous in grasp by several.

   :Is it in its social dimensions, that pure research encloses the applied world like a kernel factoring into infinite recession?

*

   ·Is it good to live so caged to name each variation of eucalyptus tree, of quantity and set, members of our band, sky, bars, man in green work shirt, visitors, dirt & sand, meager food not meant for migrants, scraps of music, stretched limbs never brought to momentum nor bath of air passed through at a run?

keeper comes with salve,
        fever lessening

listless here, two days have passed—
other animals' sound, some near,
        one so sad, it strikes me sad too

push themselves forward
        over there, over there

                    *

        raid
        another raid

        sex & grooming
        more grooming

                    *

not endogenous
        members' offspring

D: There's a regulation that experimental primates must be provisioned with exercise and entertainment. Some labs provide television.

A: Do they like it, or does it merely play in the background, waiting-room style?

D: Well, it ends up their favorite program is *Jerry Springer*. When fights break out, apparently, they get excited.

all of what it is
and more

static here
males present this, intuition into fields
                    intuits a field, a permeable space

compacted sand, a possible law, distorted plane,
ribbon candy, running stripe, crackled, quick, hot
          more hot than cold

      now that it's over, have to re-map each day
without him—no reason to save back three grapes,
no reason cricket song has sexual valence for us,
each clip a violin stutter. Once a pool of evening light

where he parked himself across from me to look hard.

Each gesture, an attenuated hand-over
had helped caption the feel

each expense of patterned sound
or temporary collection of sticks
threw up domestic
space, embankment against hygienic cages.

                    what, even with your ten thousand lives
wind, a trickster figure, rips leaf and paper litter along wall

one watches, waits
one sees
one frames

a plan in time, a fold
kept, a keeper, too:
here is my cricket, kept back in tree hole with array of sticks
          spaces set too narrow
          to come through
it chirps
just past barred light

        birds fly toward the carousel & coach house as it warms
not toward keeper's hut and storage like when it cools

        more sun
        sour taste in food, hyper-feeling
        edgy
monitors strapped here & there. I'm an experiment.

exertion, so if force and instrumentation
        make for my sovereigns
as in turn my cricket is for me

how is mind barred by them, in short
        does it participate? Can conscious sense of self

become king & queen of its own cerebrations
        ever social,
        an inter-speciation

                    *

hard not to see
visitors at railing—one big guy
lords it over others, or how that small
mean girl keeps her brother in check

        their gestures, squaring off,
        deflect, grovel—that woman who
makes her space small
in group of men

keep – O.E.D.
                        The word prob.
belonged primarily to the vulgar and
non-literary stratum of language … The
original sense may have been 'to lay hold
with the hands,' and hence with attention,
'to keep an eye upon, watch.'

keep at   (to work persistently)
keep from   (abstain)
keep to   (promise, agreement)
keep with   (remain, stay with)
keep away   (cause to remain absent)
keep back   (restrain)
keep down   (hold down in subjection)
keep in   (confine within)
keep off   (to hinder from coming near)
keep on   (maintain in an existing condition)
keep out   (cause to remain without, outside)
keep over   (reserve, hold over)
keep to   (cause a ship to sail close to the wind)
keep together   (cause to remain in association)
keep under   (to hold in subjection)
keep up   (keep shut up or contained)

meat safe, pie safe

                in locomotive engine
                part of axle-box fitted
                beneath the journal of the
                axle & serving to hold
                an oiled pad against it

Pant-laughing
pant-laughing from the exercise yard
I will help group gather and peel food later.

*

What should I name the cricket?

:This is not a cricket
:Ignore the chirp
:The great zoo escape from within
:Steal this cricket
:Being plus-one if sound counts
:See, a primate can have a pet
:Won't last long
:Looks like last year's
:Knows my every mood
:Hear me? You never listen!
:A leaping orthopterous insect, male
:The kind we make cages for
:A bug beyond compare
:Potshot at evening
:Falls silent at death
:Wants sex mostly
:Incapable of abstract thought
:Passes genetic material without trace of poetic sequence
:A guy in black suit, ultra-nude
:Leaves no trace

Keep: A Melodrama

BlazeVOX [books]
Buffalo, NY

who started that meme, that pant-laughing
is peace-making
made every day, day after day
peace, our immanent destiny
is it hard-wired in, or merely supported by our apparatus?
peace, against threat of violent pain, isolation
copy pant-laughing
our duty, our reflex

man in green work shirt
        barrel on wheels, rake

two attendants in lab coats:
        wake up from black-black time
        dressing on left arm

They decide.
Or decision itself: is government a game?

A set of rules they use
derives from another more axiomatic set—their acts
hint at how they think, constitute
ethical treatment, denial of favor, even application or
higher purpose for pain right now, my swollen arm,
yesterday's induced sleep, drawn blood, monitors

an electrode extraneous to my original set?
        my mutable electric firings …

grid of space in stacked parts
        see sky through there

could it float?
in lowered light, would each have a better shine?

nomic, immutable rules could be taken over
        by implacable face on high

:Do primates need de-bunking on paranormal claims? Big Granma's supposed ability to produce food when we need it …

:Haven't we seen others of our band positioned when door slides back and food trays slide forward?

:No tight causal relation to her—she feeds on deference. Though it may be owed, it can be challenged. And is.

A: I'm told it's a mistake to write speculative fiction. Even an omniscient narrator these days, well, you're really asking for it.

E: True, but this could be a nice little book—maybe cut that long segment.

(invocation?)

and it is in it, in it like an answer
        turn the turning thing to align the marks
        the measure
the prong, the lag, the redoubt
turn, Wheel
turn

                *

a wash
a film of light, of waves

to flatten a crystalline section to formula
        hinged
in a jointure of mirrors
slice of mental space, corner sunk

School for Perisarcous Considerations

Turned fully down, a new socket, felt farm: what is
felt for lint, language for an existential quantifier,
        elevated stanchions for sacrifice. Such

was industrial revolution rooted
in nomadism, rock-perch, and coal fire; such

was postmodernism rooted
in shift-pattern, delivery failure, and gladiatorial spiff; such

was modernism rooted
in drafting conventions, vertical reprise, and dirty dreams; such

was romanticism rooted
in answers to being called, floral swords, and machine-free cloth.

(Note: look into www.chimphaven.org, the facility to retire chimpanzees from medical
protocol, entertainment industry, or no longer wanted as pets)

Overly tuned to regularity's
        methods, they roll their instrumental

cart right over
with something tight

back to you.

                *

Something contained and air,
        how squeeze structures

direction
        taking on perfume
        inside me.

                *

The drain in our savannah simulacrum
        is plugged with leaves.

                        Actual, dead.
Cement channel.

Where they held ambulant toy or finance capital
                              ape-belly

whose long arms seem now so slack
                    carry maybe
                    carry could

we saw opals, thought: hot springs.
                    They had
sheeted rain from standing-seam metal roofs
          exerted force on protesters, killed seven,
as they had it out with allegorized truth.

heavy rain, all sent inside

loud, loud
            Will
we fall out
of our shadows?

            Will the ending then
hesitate a bit
right through here? Your puddle.

                              Lab again, what to see?
same arrangement—each grid in packing crate
three to one side
four to the other
                         openings
hand-holds, two

       :But then you see it's not about inventory, *Principia*, or any sort of complete
directory with items and variant relations,

       it's how to represent generative proximities and iterative engines that jump
tracks to move onto irregular landscapes.

press on

earn my keep

REM sleep:

I'm running at full extension of my arms and legs.

There seems to be a purpose.

Upon arriving to a clearing, startled birds fly upward.

Their formation tells me, right away, there are 240.

As soon as I grasp this formula, the birds are gone.

Somehow I began to fall.

Falling in what seemed infinitely slow time, an electric charge circulated at top speed around my head three times.

I'm aware of a burnt smell then woke here strapped to the gurney.

A lab attendant leaned over to look into my eyes.

Promycelium, a lesser word's underbelly

Baroque folds, unending sense of *more*, envelopment.
They use a way to look from behind a Polaroid visor,
a helmet, is it you? Neither original nor cloth surrogate,
this cube has found me, subtle scar tissue just here.
To hear your prepared words, a gift, for sure.
We might not be able to name all information
on offer to our brains, but pattern-recognition suits us.

            By blunt force object
or electrocardiogram. Oh, the bright communications
satellite at eastern horizon, felt folds, or wrapped coast.
Triangulating from the Naval Weapons base even with
moonlight, I can see it clearly over sinuous forms,
hermit of motherboards' silver qualities, minimalism's
haggle with baroque, another idealization of star surfaces:
spherical, equivalent in temperature across its expanses.

How, the means

after Bill Viola's video installation entitled *Fall into Paradise* from his larger work *LOVE/DEATH: The Tristan Project* that was invited by the Paris National Opera for its production of Wagner's *Tristan und Isolde* (1865)

I apply
so you

            how
underneath, what does this say
what does this want to say about want

you see
blouse opening

I see you see

back centuries, their
fall into Paradise

                                  how
have we modified the garden,

has it done us—
I have no words

the means, haptic

yet thrum
black duet

      how
re-mastered
chanson, arteries

rapid climb
your nonvocable

on the plain

expand evenly

who knows
who we are now

—or the solo
his squared
off chest

held by salt sea, how oxygen,
will return upward

how with us common air
pierced the sea

        close the lid
light skirmishes there

rib-pattern
off and on

(who)
when you rode
to see
where I am

you found a copy
you thought would work

asunder, that city
ordinary message

taken
on the plain, evenly
page screened there

        how is where,
our chorus has means
to mean

pariah, it comes down
where do you go?

named in the meeting room
       violence: being a topic

marked

our island, meek
can we paddle there

read a play?

If I turn back
I see you
          They set a look:
how stage is seen,
these many points

fanned out
drawn back up

retracted inside itself

are you destroyed
by multiplication—small pieces

shame thrown on

your letter

how I needed it

      open to come,
comes back
your look
more and more
our separateness
in privacy
seen already
I empty
slip
your being over
me
your being there, here
make susceptible
how we
sequence

not saying so
there, here

                how priests
keep us from being
gods, their formula

holy bodies, said,
know an ancient knowing

somatic inscription
marked here
            on him
            on me

for mind, said,
pleasure left
pungent word
(re-staged here)

               how
       preside over
end of it
end it here

potion, poison
chance, plan
tremble to bring it within

freed result, pairing:
his shelter, my cut

put on, put in

surface we crave
surface we lean in toward

                    by sweat,
by the exit
from it

you know the room
I'm in, hour

the little said,
not the sense of things
to which you are accustomed

threat
impending here—
a dense curtain
            that can
            mow down

to the ear
an object of attention

somehow: refrain

its recurrence
a sort of code
for our passion

force,
your magnificent

what proof requires
what torment for inconsequential
words, but of three:

just thrown down
erected edifice
cloud-envelope

night over too soon
regained his pants, shirt, etc.

said, hasty
breathing breath

imitations
you plant yourself
a perch, wait
to see me

I walk there
every other day, how:
bring ship-wrecked parts
to form a raft
so save
eros from resembling
escape

not sturdy, these
found objects

he wades into
a great internal design
soon to structure his world

I enfold.

Not a fall, at first,
how interpret?

release, second
we are released,
fall, fallen
come to

             (breathe)
scatter pieces

how they come to contain

the paper, not the words, material to shred

no way to un-
confound, defend
as far different
from cliché of it then.

Later readers
as they tear into it,
          match names and desire,
see.

                    war continued
despite our sanctuary

if I listened

inside I would hesitate
                    hear
the world sound
authoritative—

shot sub-surface

        highways out
        to desert
proving grounds

movement toward
an uncovered origin,
outlandish control

Why are we here
where it's hot?

where, a site index

The new head-up display

allows user to view airspeed and angle
of attack on transparent display without
requiring user to look away from windshield
        down to flight
        instruments, and
computes gunnery solutions for user
especially in air to air battles, i.e., dogfights

With hand on joystick

how Synthetic Vision technologies train pilots
how technologies adjust pictorial format and focus
how virtual reality helps re-train severely injured military personnel
how the use of GPS and Intertial Reference Systems solve navigation problems
how we are no longer flying blind
how 3D technologies with conventional perspective give pilots an "intuitive" feel for
    their flying environments
how the new boresight symbol (- V -) is in the center, and the horizon line shows pitch
how the Tunnel in the Sky is a conceptualization of flight paths depicted by vision
    systems
how Enhanced Vision uses near-infrared cameras and millimeter wave radar in limited
    visibility environments
how head-up display (HUD) with predicted impact point (PIP) helps pilots make
    accurate hits with ballistic projectiles
how a glowing red dot appears over the weapon's impact point regardless of the
    shooter's eye position
how saccades help rods and cones refresh an image read by the brain, create continuity
how synthetic vision is used for Remotely Piloted Vehicles (RPVs) with control signals
    up-linked and aircraft telemetry down-linked to remote cockpit displays
how Synthetic Vision systems could have prevented the crash of American Airlines
    Flight 965 in 1995
how helmet mounted displays (HMD) move with the user's head relative to the airframe
how new experiments attempt HUD systems that project information on the inside of
    swimmer's goggles
how new experiments attempt HUD systems that project information onto the wearer's
    retina with a low-powered laser
how HUD designers consider that a person's eyes are at two different points and seek
    to prevent a person from re-focusing between display and outside world
how designers attempt to accurately map display onto what the pilot sees
how altitude and speed are your friend when trying to deal with "unexpected events."

Weak as a directive, no

Weak as a directive, no vivid allegory
of bones-to-resurrection, thimblomachy, but
toy-cute, is the miniature an after-effect where the mechanism
might be a vast amount of text, say Leviticus
or Kama Sutra, inscribed on a caraway seed so
you need magnifying apparatus to read
ligature of plants, priests, and positions per seed surface?

Ekphrastic-generated streets held fancies and delights in line,
as well as slums and mufti despair, vying for dominance:
what group is more exclusive?
      Is it a pitchfork or a metonymic framework,
but no, it's the old *City of Quartz* story after all, the West
built by developers, disbelievers in public space,
who work their predatory boredom, a dynastic speed-up

in relation to populace. The hypothetical city each carries,
well-lit space, etc. in thrice-viewed movie, embrace of
gods fresh from Wardrobe whose grey buildings and
crowded sidewalks out-lurid our own origins, our own
sense of nothingness, so scan for departures from first
plan as if Cenozoic weight could shift us from paucity
of settlement, dented tin globe, Celestine rot not about
aerialists in crenellated domes or chimps in space, our
proxies might not latch shut helmet and deluxe harness,
might not take it anymore.

dynastic speed-up

Resorts to Quinoidine substitutions

So, here, dump Rio explicitly, charge the film's
orthogonals who recognized kids' segregation
     in print that p.m., hundreds of events in voice-over
lamely tried for a humoresque run at political things, actively offer
     the impoverished situation a joke, yuk
at the expense of scavengers, drug-traffickers
     in favelas of New York, throw down a bus
load choked to death, two very recently
     near a child witness police evaluate
psychologically for reason, money, inescapability
     of hardship, so crafted a reading of news
could be a naturalistic novel whose purpose
     dissipates as determined lives of drug lords,
client states where product emerges run to stereotype,
     ethnographic Inferno.

"to super dense star"

            a picaresque take on totality against detective
or pedantic work
            the little customs, afoot with an appetitive imperative
that drives general deep into particular, connoisseurship.

Took a cue from the French for vignettes that satirize
        citified pomposities, moral inclusions,
a long cerebral wrinkle set with pathology,
        "natural" speech, degenerate line of descent, walls.

                                    Once a struggle
        with an angel, now a heap of parts recoverable
only partially and with great effort against unified effect.

                            We, the deracinated.

    The precedent here seems to recede to shadowy
allusion perhaps fabricated, utopian, post-dated
        so it can be honored in "our context," fire
regulations, authoritarian parade of what are really
        structural supports without much added meaning
        minus this display, commentary, gross lighting.

Sagittate Leaves

architecture by installment, feuilleton pieces
        sociological subscription
        works by train

striking, all these workers, below scriptural images

tally, genealogy, ironic defense of observant ones
        "reading" the situation
                        The last
aphorism is a generic name for book-making

                -ence
                -ian
                -eet
                -adt

famished chinstraps coming of age, mournful studies
        of back formations, agents of mortality.

Deborah Meadows lives in the Arts District/Little Tokyo section of Los Angeles with Howard Stover. She teaches in the Liberal Studies department at California State Polytechnic University, Pomona. Her Electronic Poetry Center author page is located: http://epc.buffalo.edu/authors/meadows/